W9-AYM-744

Ayudantes de la comunidad / Helping the Community

¿Qué hacen LOS POLICÍAS?
What Do POLICE OFFICERS Do?

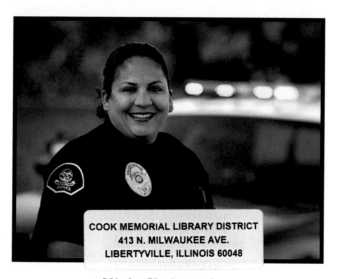

Nick Christopher
Traducido por Eida de la Vega

PowerKiDS
press.

New York

Published in 2016 by The Rosen Publishing Group, Inc.
29 East 21st Street, New York, NY 10010

First Edition

Editor: Katie Kawa
Book Design: Katelyn Heinle
Spanish Translator: Eida de la Vega

Photo Credits: Cover (police officer), p. 1 Blend Images - Hill Street Studios/Brand X Pictures/Getty Images; cover (hands) bymandesigns/Shutterstock.com; series back cover Zffoto/Shutterstock.com; pp. 5, 14 © iStockphoto.com/kali9; pp. 6, 21 John Roman Images/Shutterstock.com; p. 9 Peter Dazeley/Iconica/Getty Images; pp. 10, 24 (uniform) pio3/Shutterstock.com; p. 13 © iStockphoto.com/shaunl; p. 17 Carolina K. Smith MD/Shutterstock.com; pp. 18, 24 (siren) Kant Komalasnangkoon/Shutterstock.com; p. 22 Karsten Bidstrup/Lonely Planet Images/Getty Images.

Library of Congress Cataloging-in-Publication Data

Christopher, Nick.
 What do police officers do? = ¿Qué hacen los policías? / Nick Christopher.
    pages cm. — (Helping the community = Ayudantes de la comunidad)
Parallel title: Ayudantes de la comunidad.
In English and Spanish.
 Includes bibliographical references and index.
ISBN 978-1-4994-0615-3 (library binding)
1. Police—Juvenile literature. I. Title.
HV7922.C47 2016
363.2—dc23

Manufactured in the United States of America

CPSIA Compliance Information: Batch #WS15PK: For Further Information contact Rosen Publishing, New York, New York at 1-800-237-9932

CONTENIDO

CONTENTS

Los policías mantienen a salvo a las personas.

Police officers help people stay safe.

CROSS POLICE LINE DO NOT

Los policías se aseguran de que la gente obedezca las leyes. Las leyes son reglas importantes.

Police officers make sure people follow laws. Laws are important rules.

Los policías también ayudan a los niños que se pierden.

Police officers also help kids who are lost.

Los policías usan una ropa que se llama **uniforme**.

Police officers wear clothes called a **uniform**.

¡Los autos de los policías corren a mucha velocidad!

Police officers drive cars that can go fast!

Los policías paran a
las personas que manejan
muy rápido.

Police officers stop people
when they are driving too fast.

Los autos de policía tienen luces en el techo. Las luces son rojas y azules.

Police cars have lights on the top. The lights are red and blue.

SIRENA
SIREN

Los autos de policía tienen una **sirena**. Las sirenas hacen mucho ruido.

Police cars have a **siren**. Sirens make loud noises.

Algunos policías trabajan con perros.

Some police officers work with dogs.

¡Los policías son muy serviciales!

Police officers are very helpful!

PALABRAS QUE DEBES APRENDER
WORDS TO KNOW

(la) sirena
siren

(el) uniforme
uniform

ÍNDICE / INDEX

SITIOS DE INTERNET / WEBSITES

Due to the changing nature of Internet links, PowerKids Press has developed an online list of websites related to the subject of this book. This site is updated regularly. Please use this link to access the list: www.powerkidslinks.com/htc/pol